**Library of Congress Cataloging-in-Publication Data**
The Phantom copyright (c) 1989 King Features Syndicate, Inc. All rights reserved. This book copyright (c) 1989 by Pioneer Books, Inc. All rights reserved. Published by Pioneer Books, Inc., 5715 N. Balsam Rd., Las Vegas, NV, 89130.
International Standard Book Number: 1-55698-250-X    First Printing 1989

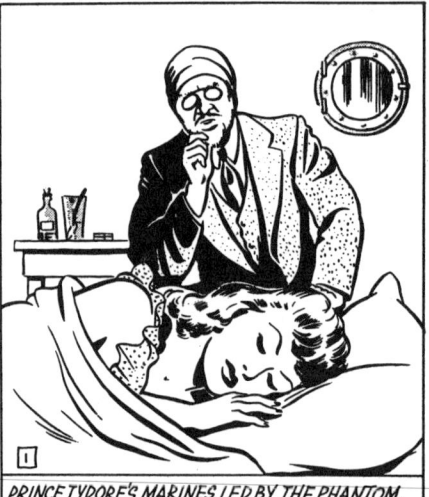

»

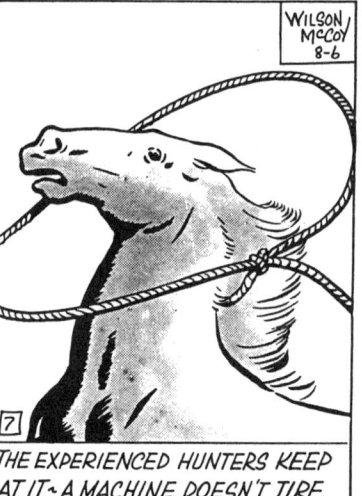

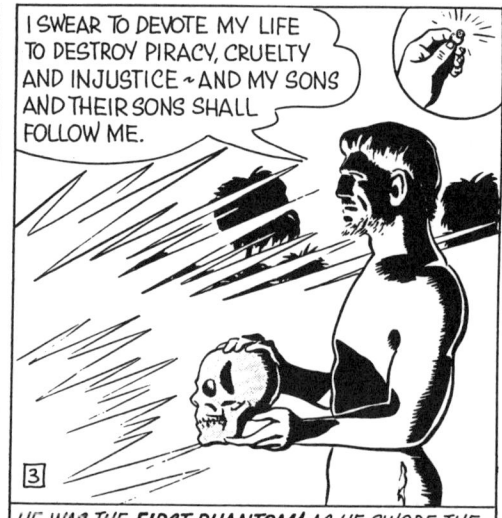

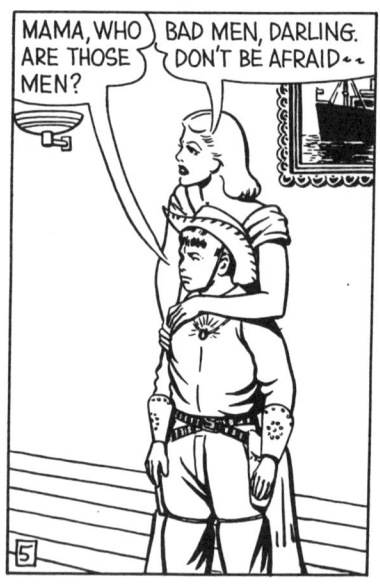

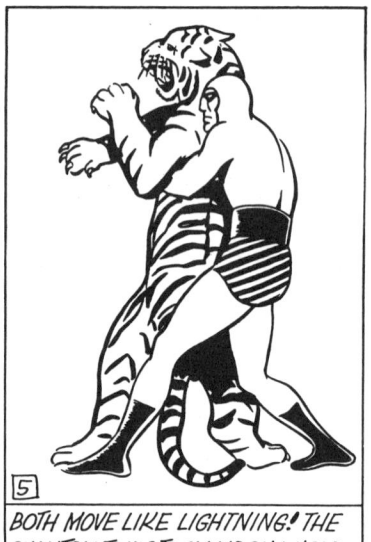

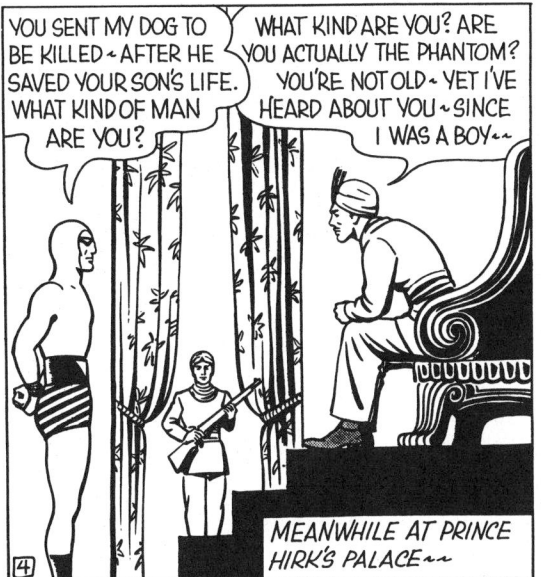

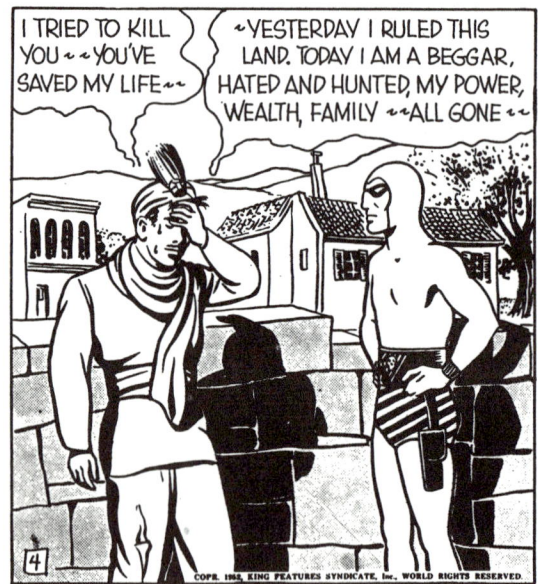

# EXCITING EARLY ISSUES!

If your local comic book specialty store no longer has copies of the early issues you may want to order them directly from us.

**By Roy Crane:**
\_Buz Sawyer #1 \_Buz Sawyer #2 \_Buz Sawyer #3 \_Buz Sawyer #4 \_Buz Sawyer #5

**By Alex Raymond:**
\_Jungle Jim 1 \_Jungle Jim 2 \_Jungle Jim 3 \_Jungle Jim 4 \_Jungle Jim 5 \_Jungle Jim 6 \_Jungle Jim 7
\_Rip Kirby #1 \_Rip Kirby #2 \_Rip Kirby #3 \_Rip Kirby #4

**By Lee Falk and Phil Davis:**
\_Mandrake #1 \_Mandrake #2 \_Mandrake #3 \_Mandrake #4 \_Mandrake #5 \_Mandrake #6 \_Mandrake #7

**By Hal Foster:**
\_P V #1 \_P V #2 \_P V #3 \_P V #4 \_P V #5 \_P V #6 \_P V #7 \_P V #8 \_P V AN. ($5.00)

**By Archie Goodwin and Al Williamson:**
\_Secret Agent #1 \_Secret Agent #2 \_Secret Agent #3 \_Secret Agent #4 \_Secret Agent #5 \_Secret Agent #6

(All about the heroes including interviews with Hal Foster, Lee Falk and Al Williamson:)
\_ THE KING COMIC HEROES   $14.95
(The following two book-size collections preserve the original strip format)
\_ THE MANDRAKE SUNDAYS   $14.95
\_ THE PHANTOM SUNDAYS   $14.95
\_ THE JUNGLE JIM SUNDAYS   $14.95
\_ THE RIP KIRBY DAILIES   $12.95

\_ (Enclosed) Please enclose $3.00 per comic ordered and/or $17.95 for THE KING COMIC HEROES and/or $14.95 for THE MANDRAKE SUNDAYS. and/or $14.95 for THE JUNGLE JIM SUNDAYS and/or $14.95 for THE PHANTOM SUNDAYS and/or $12.95 for THE RIP KIRBY DAILIES. Shipping and handling are included.

Name: _____

Street: _____

City: _____

State: _____

Zip Code: _____
Check or money order only. No cash please. All payments must be in US funds. Please add $5.00 to foreign orders.
I remembered to enclose:$_____

Please send to:
Pioneer, 5715 N. Balsam Rd., Las Vegas, NV 89130